Color More
&
Stress Less

ADULT COLORING BOOK

www.colormorestressless.com

by Star Miller-Becerra

Introduction

Coloring is very therapeutic, and allows you to relieve stress, anxiety and even tap into your creative side.

These detailed Kaleidoscope style pictures will give you a challenging, yet relaxing way to spend a few min or a few hours every day.

Where to start?
If you don't know where you'd like to start, here are some tips...

Close your eyes and pick any colored pencil, gel pen or crayon.
What color did you pick? Red? Blue? Black? Pink? Green? Yellow?

Close your eyes again and touch your color on the page anywhere.
This is where you will start!

Now color! Yes, Color! You remember how to color right? We learned how to do this in Kindergarten. I know, I know, it's been a while. For some of us longer than others (I am in that boat too)! In a few minutes you will start to see your masterpiece come to life!

TIPS: Stay with it. Create a new habit! Make it a regular practice while eating your breakfast or right after dinner. Perhaps right before bed is your favorite time to unwind.

Whatever time of day works for you, as you make it more and more of a habit, you will experience less stress, less anxiety and more enjoyable and positive changes in your life. Everyone's results are unique to their situation, though we'd love to hear your stories and see your work of art!   Visit us at:

www.ColorMoreStressLess.com

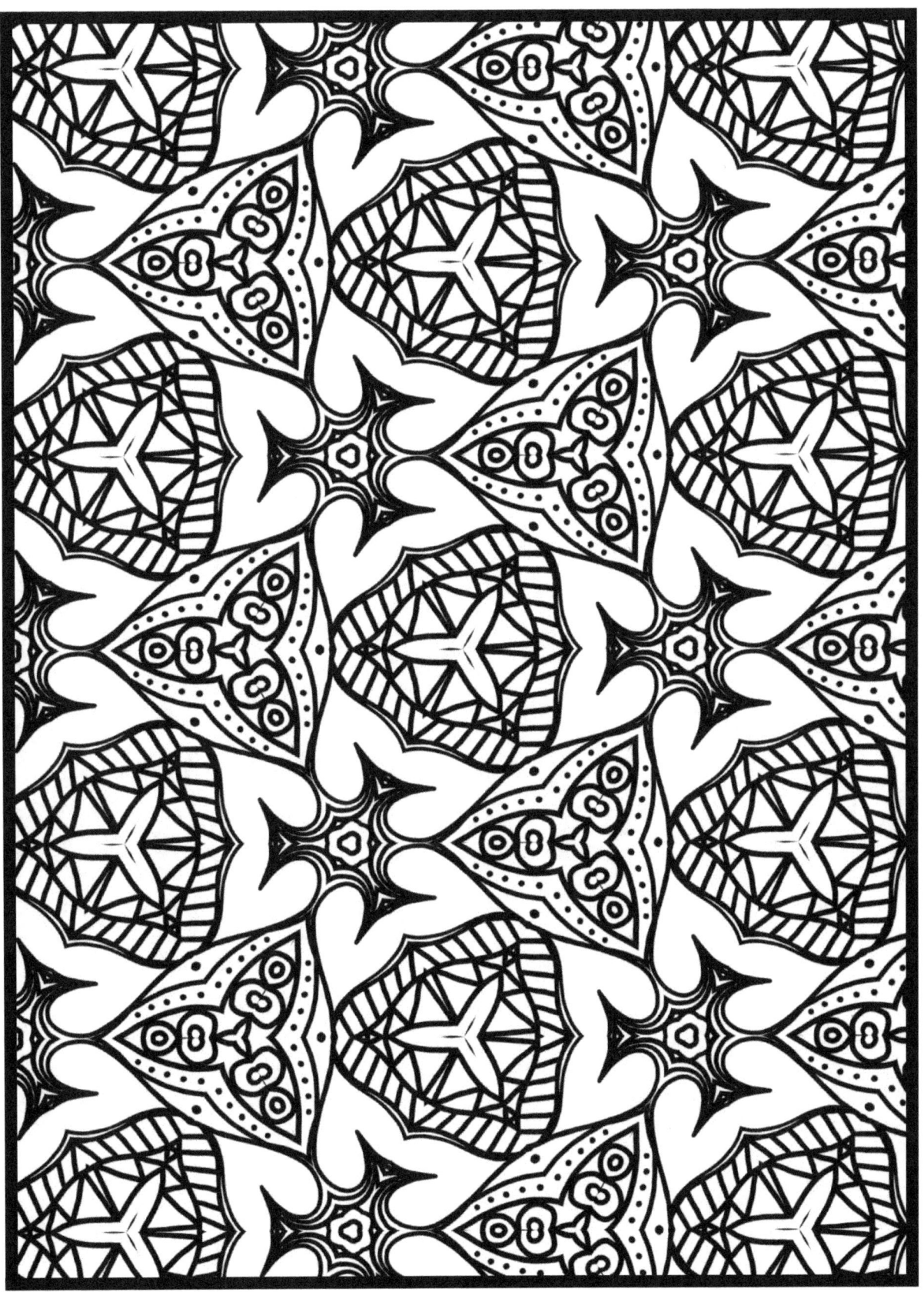

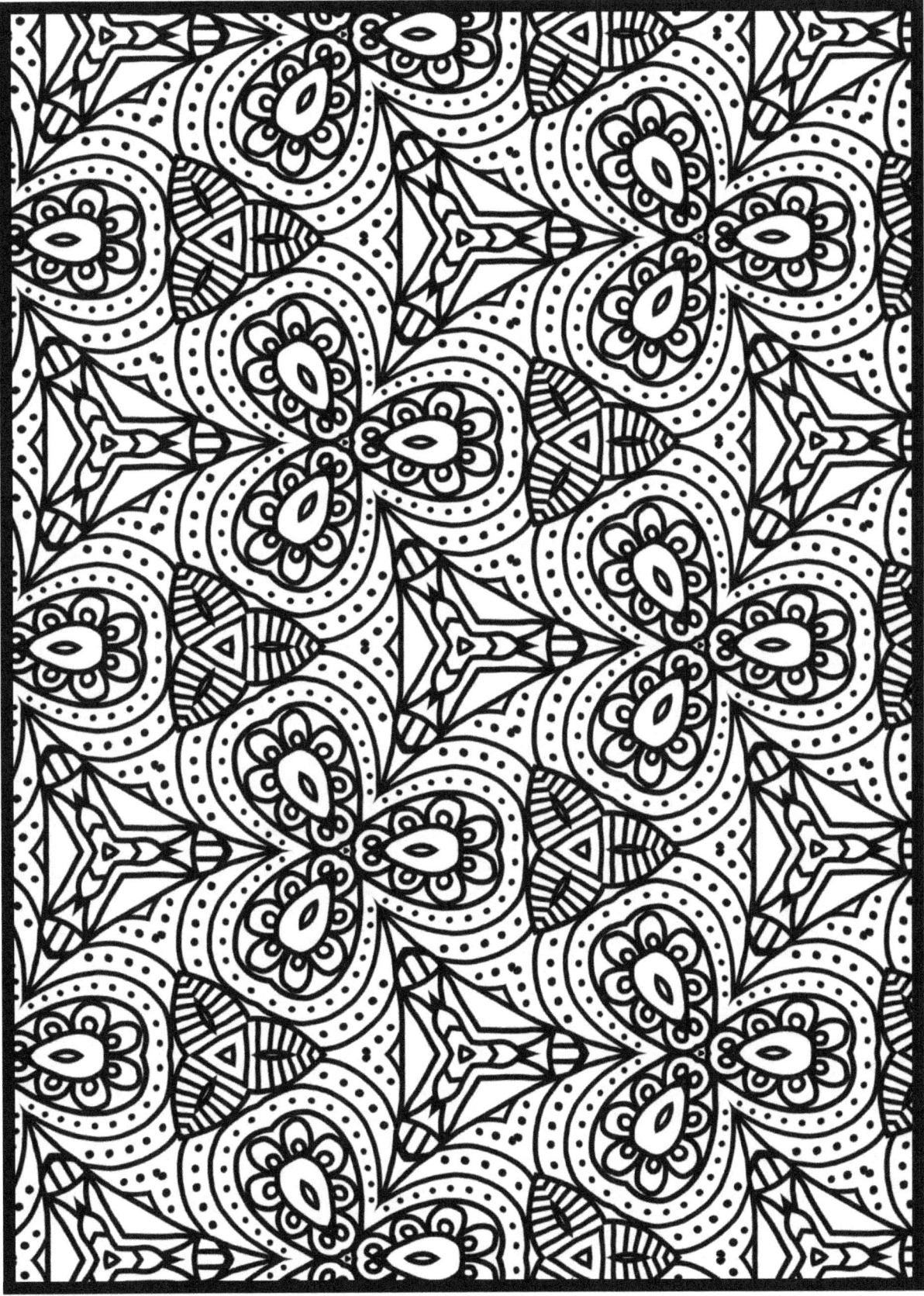

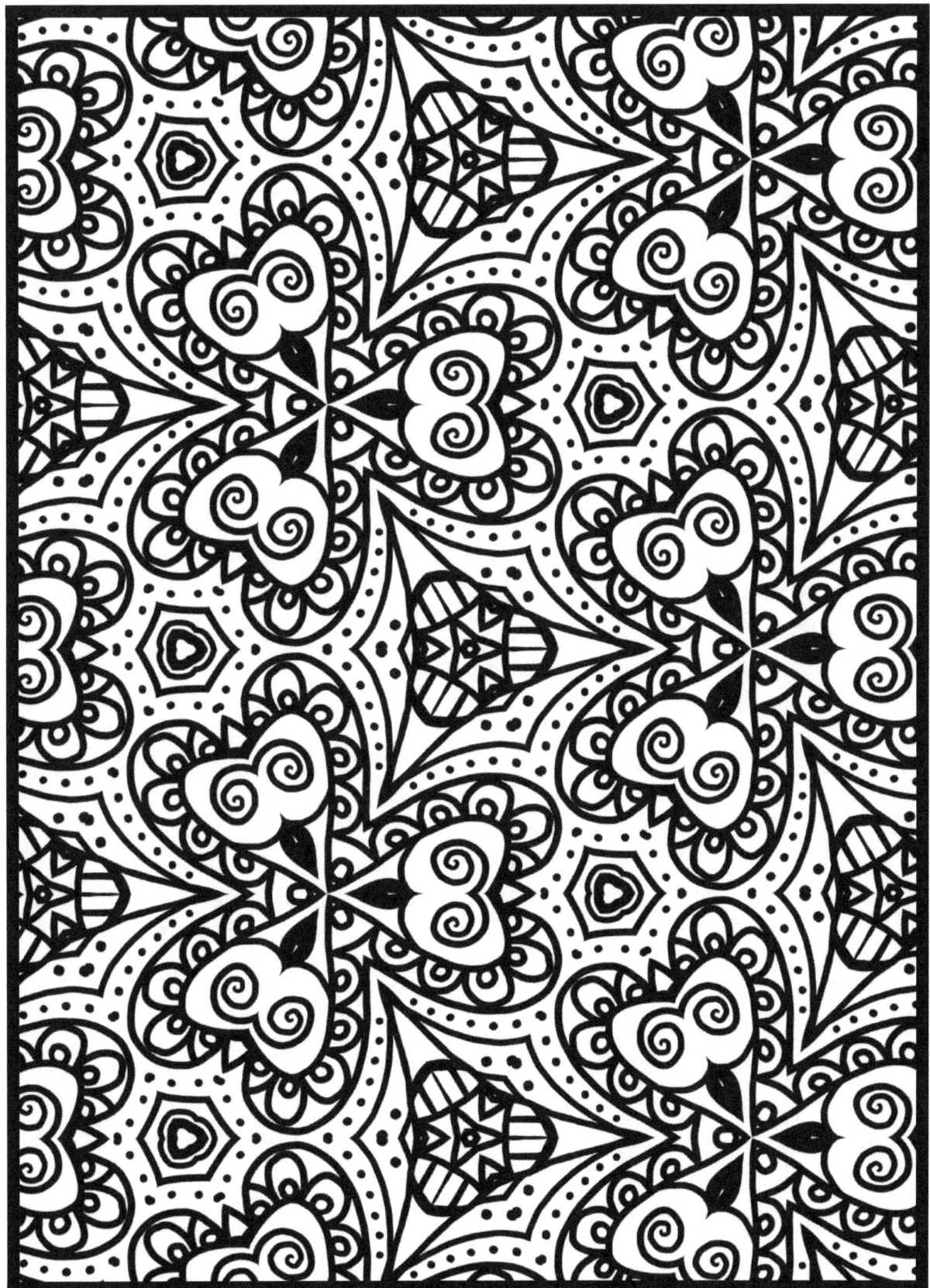

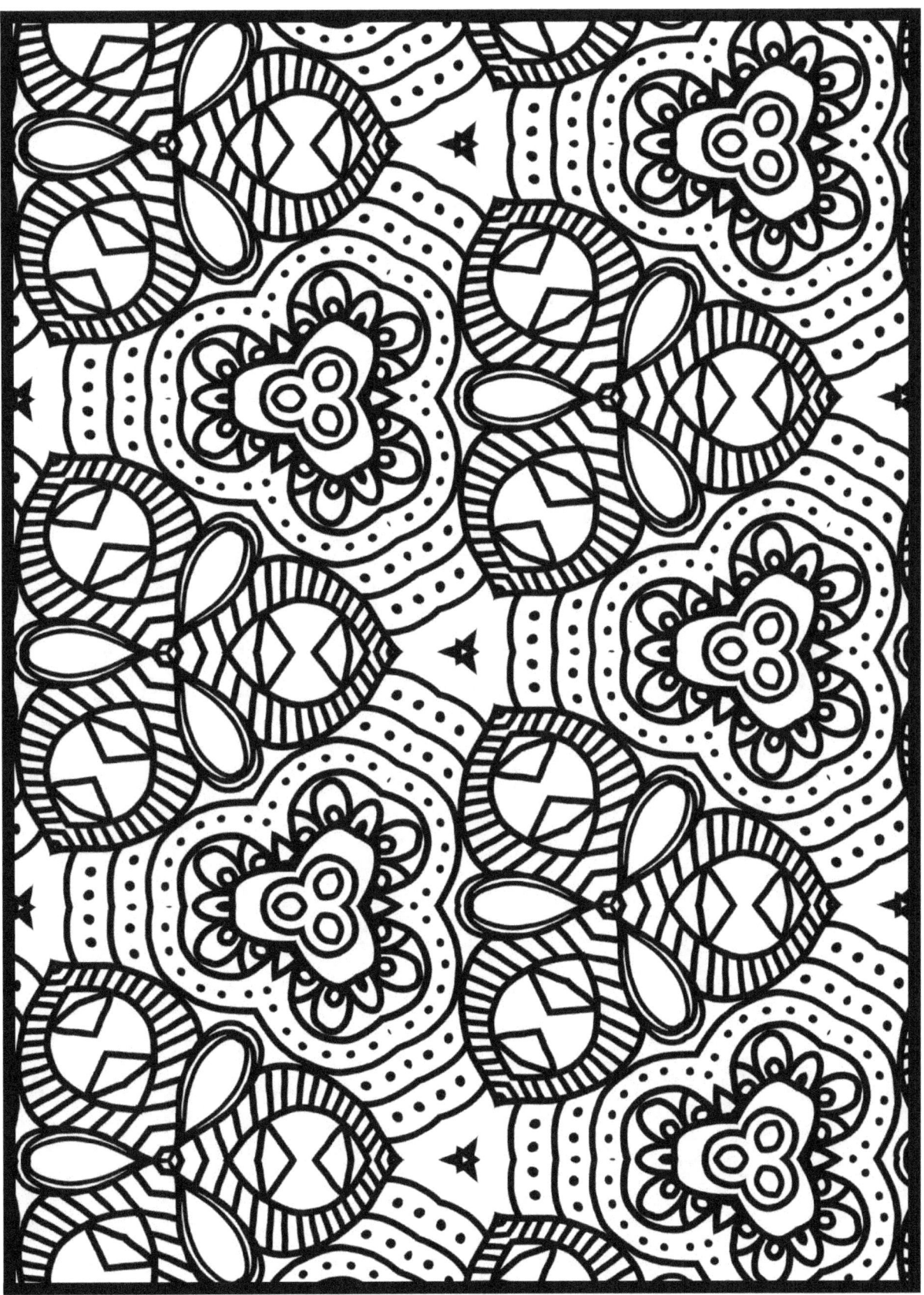

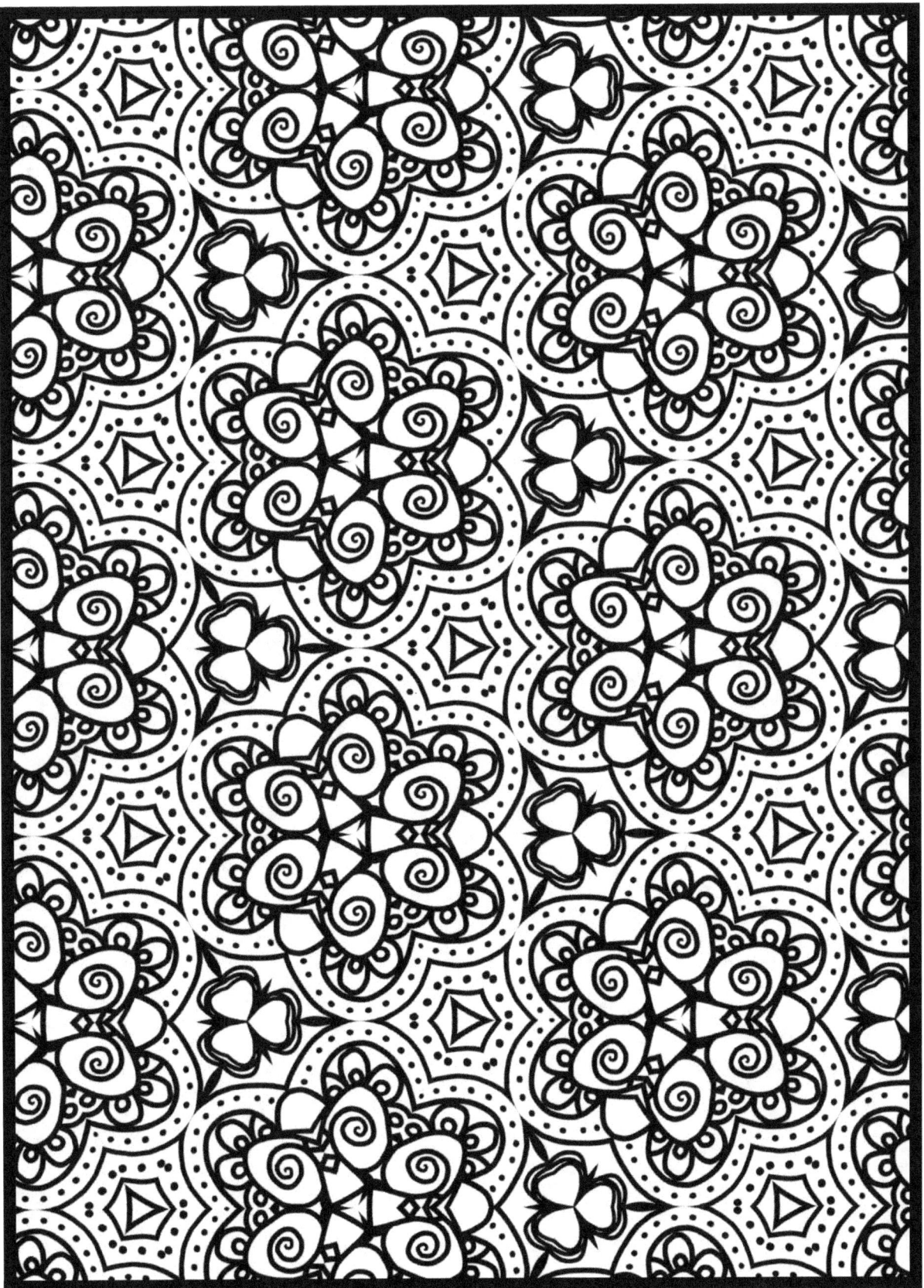

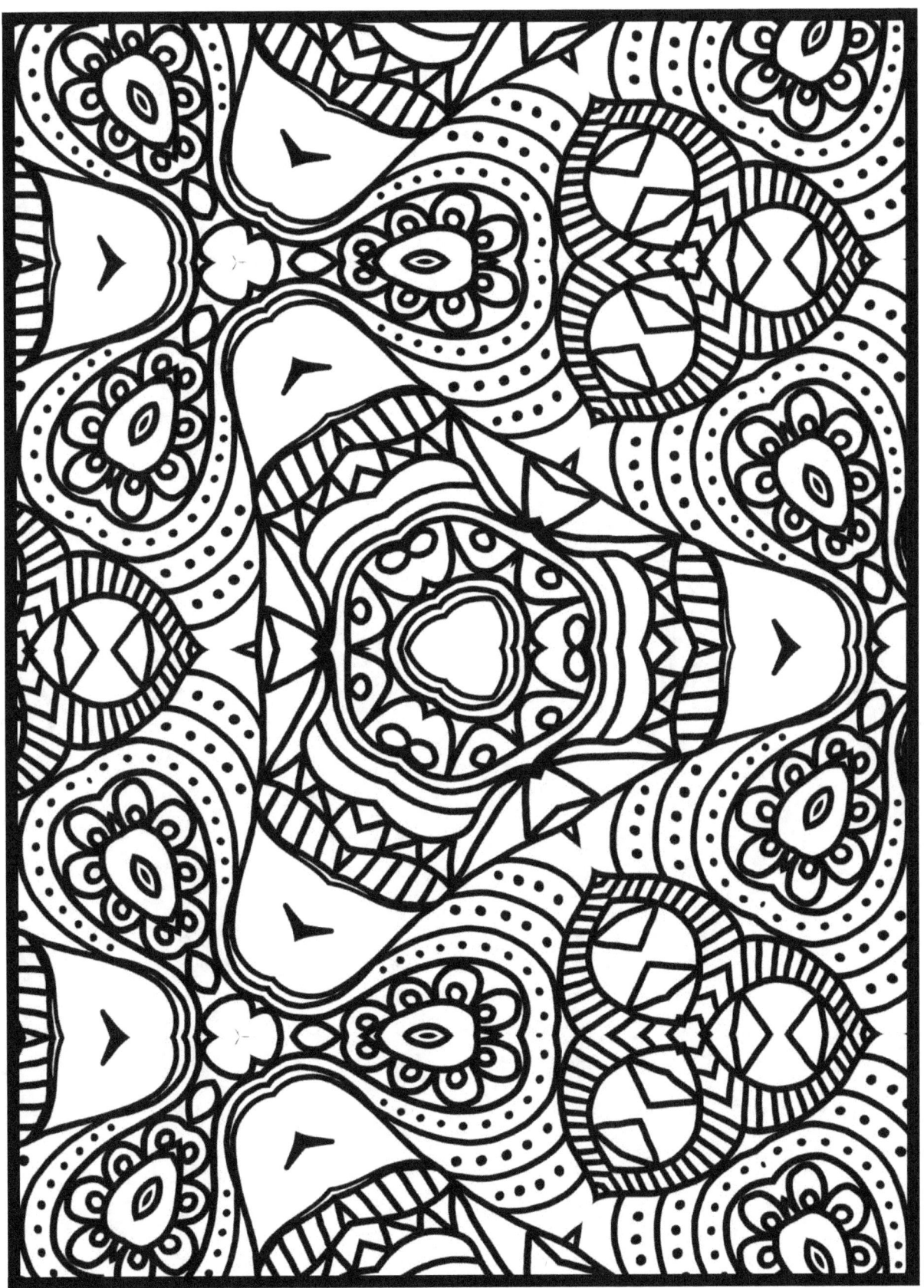

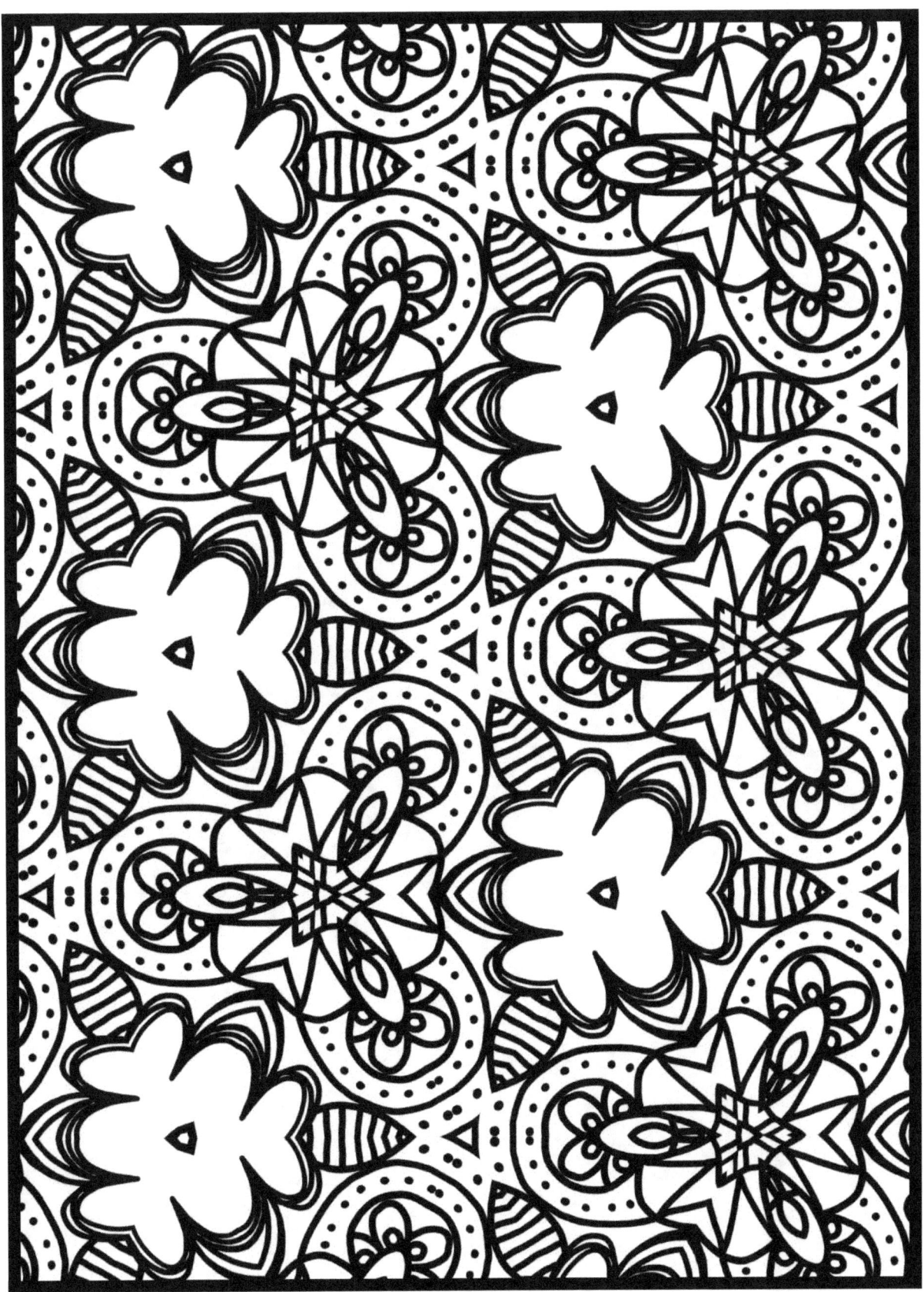

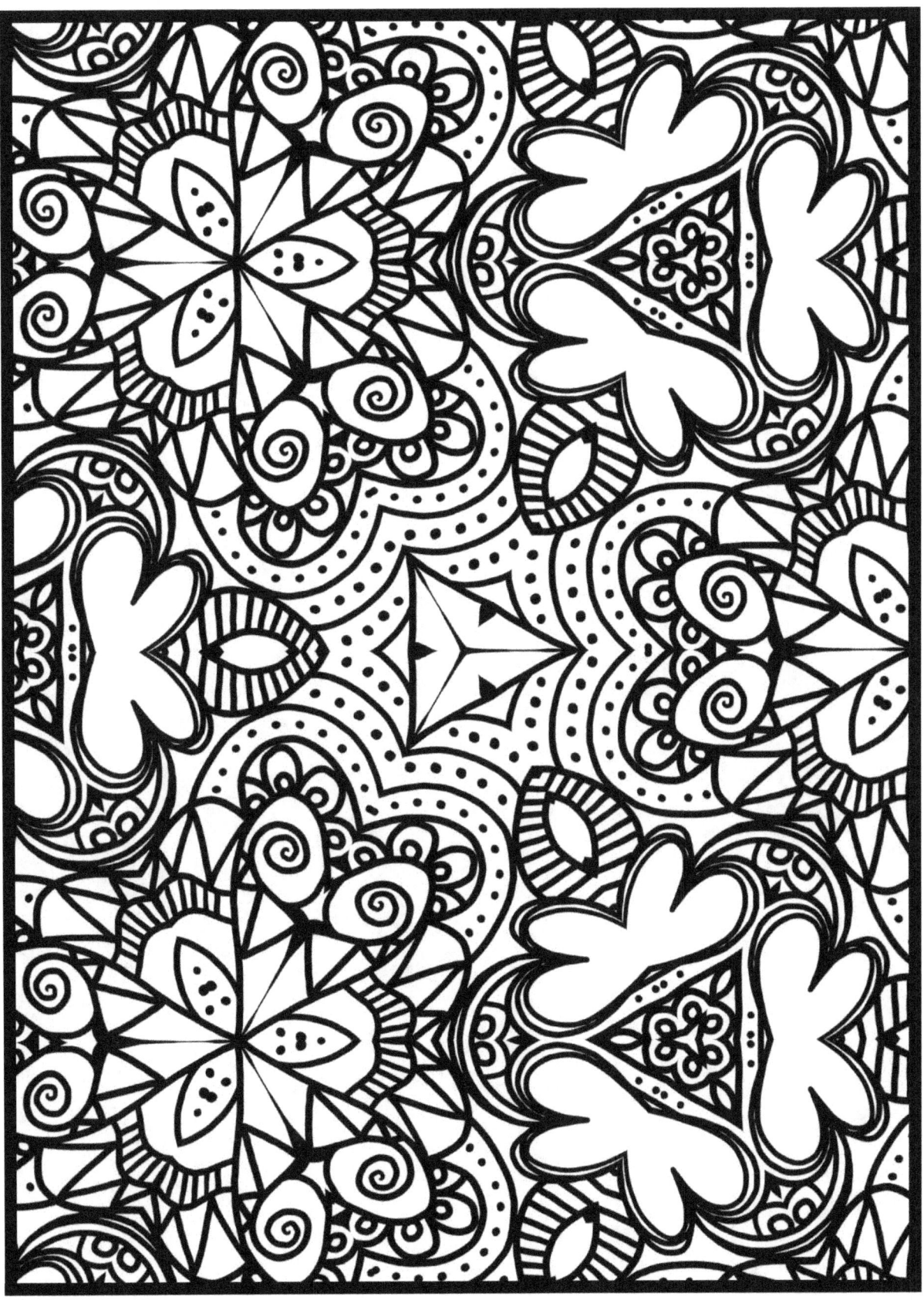

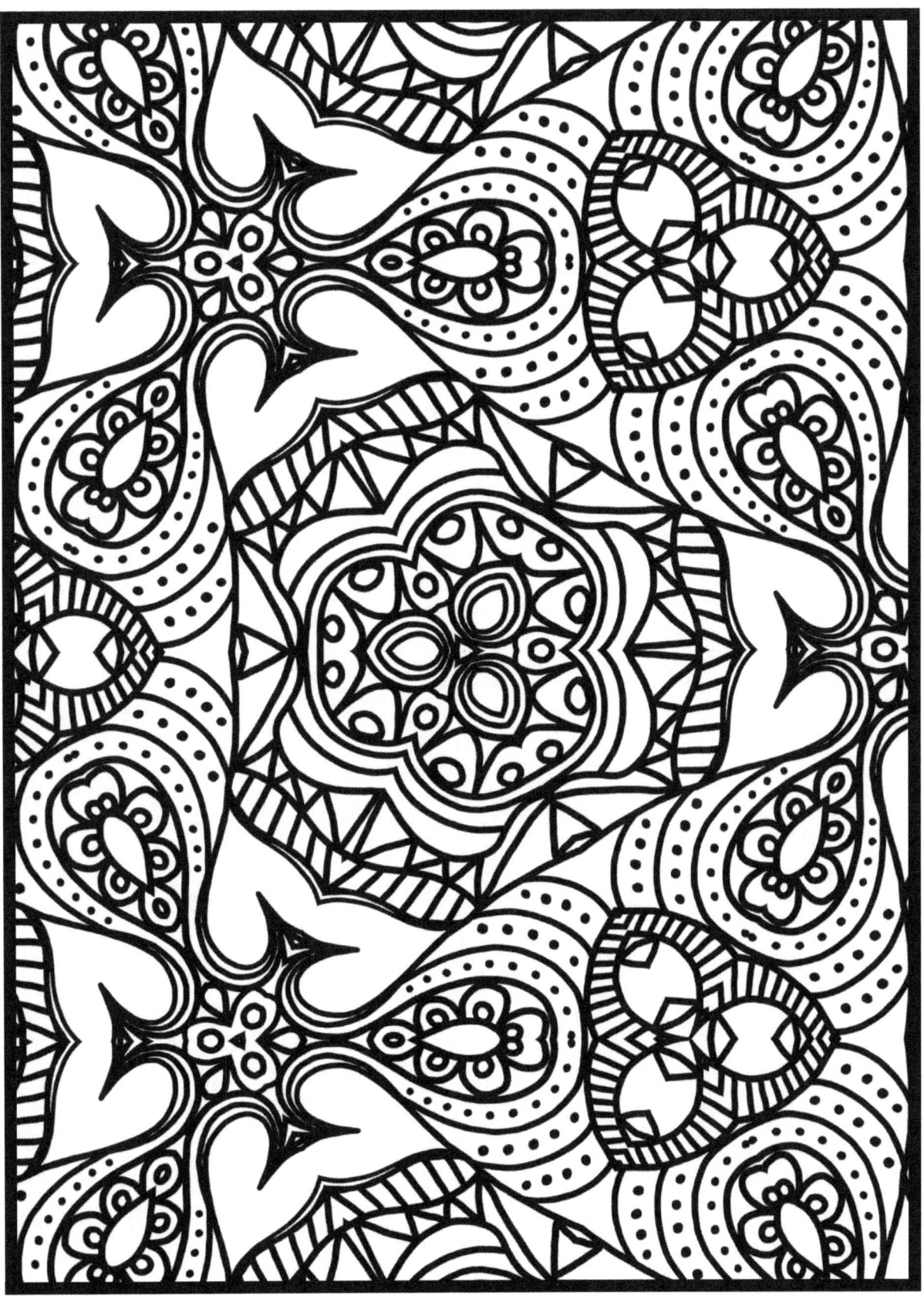

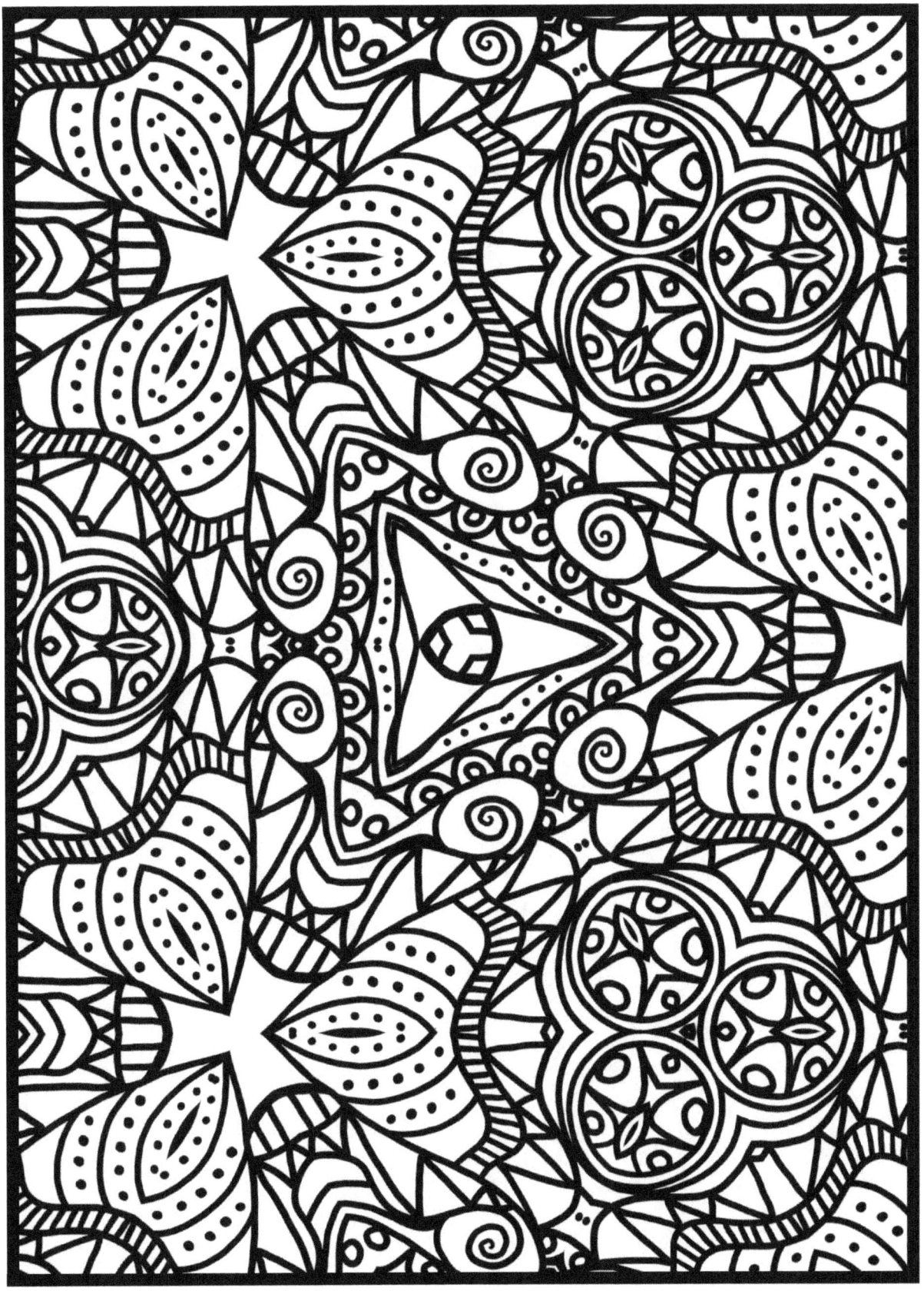

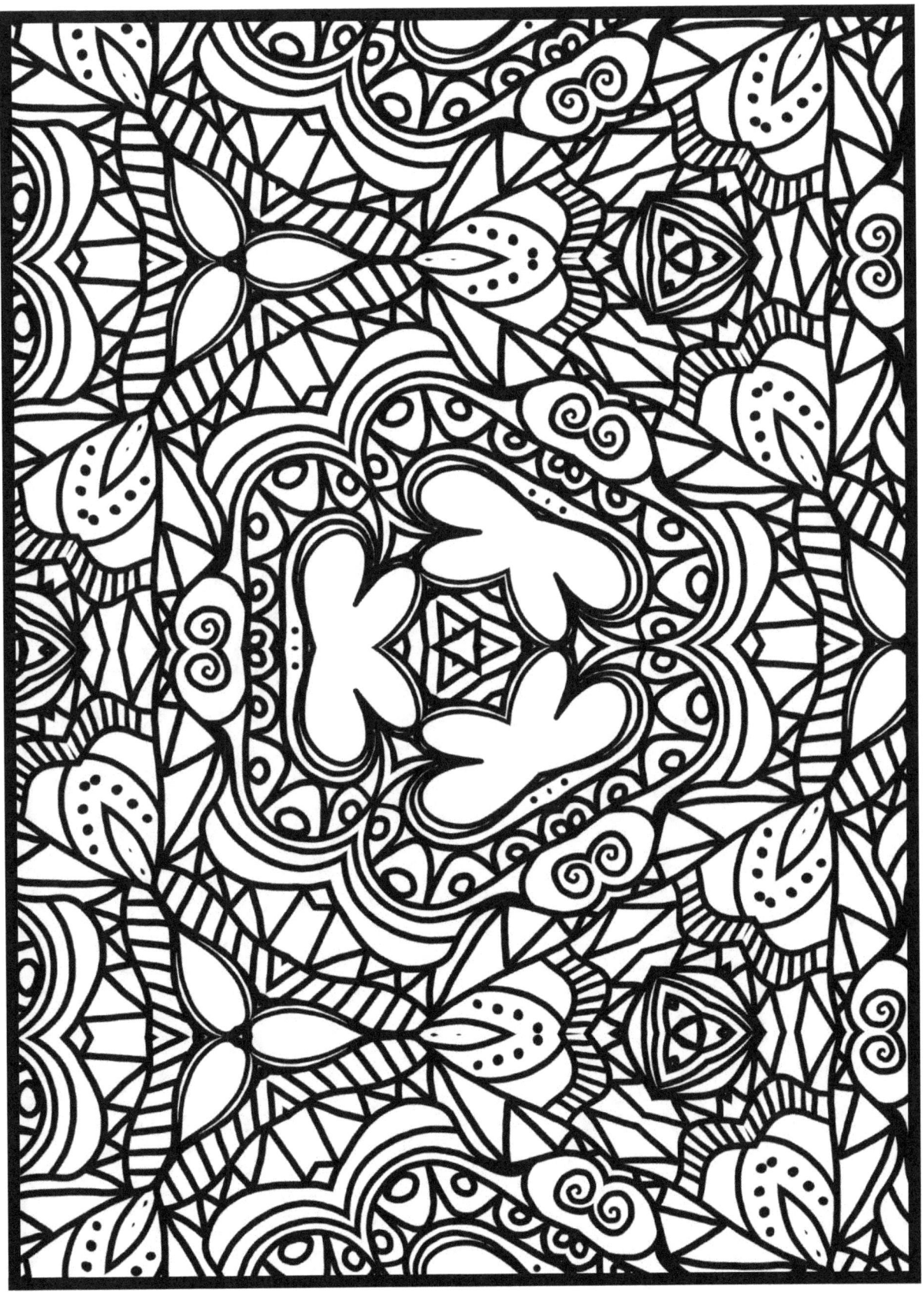

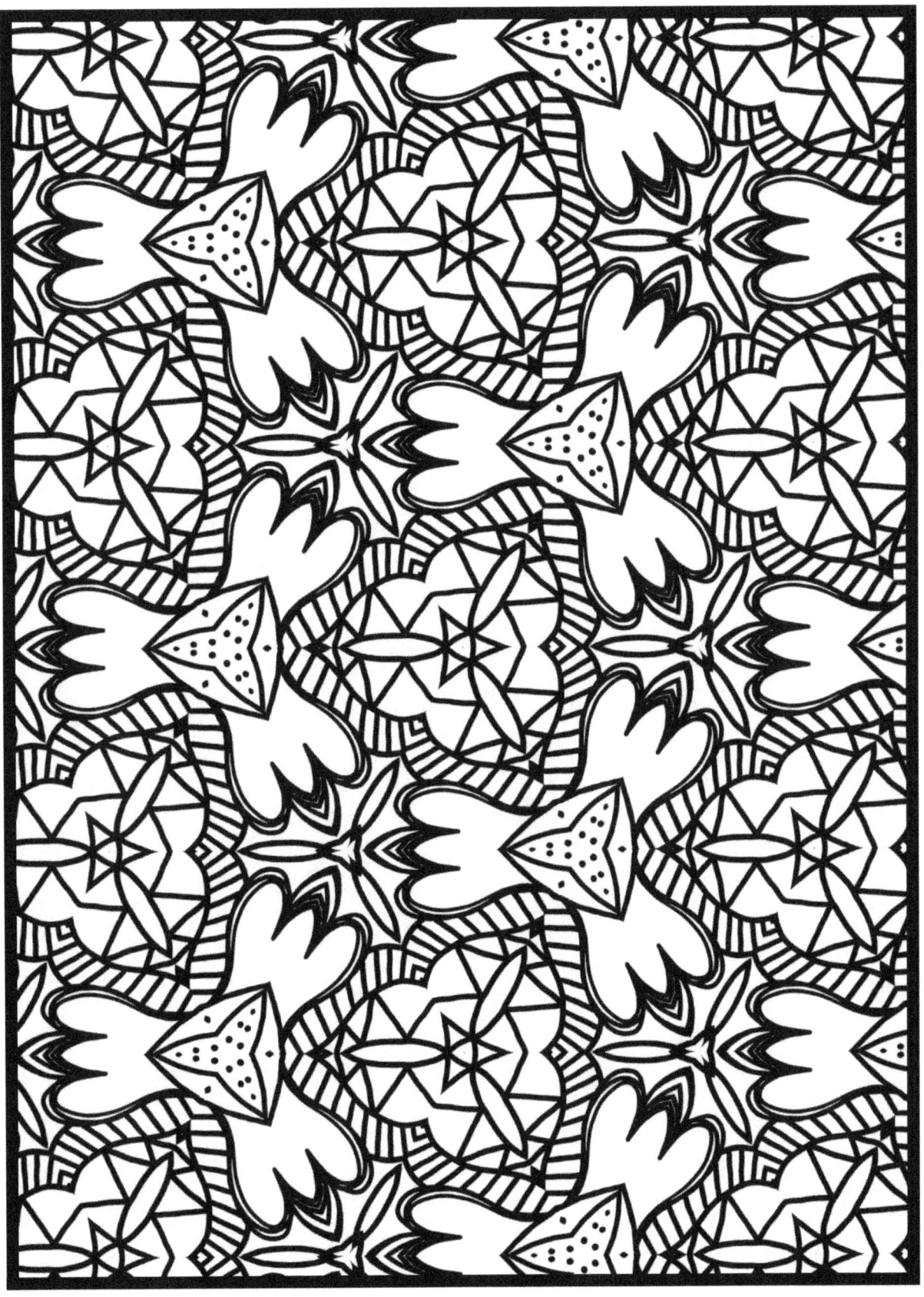

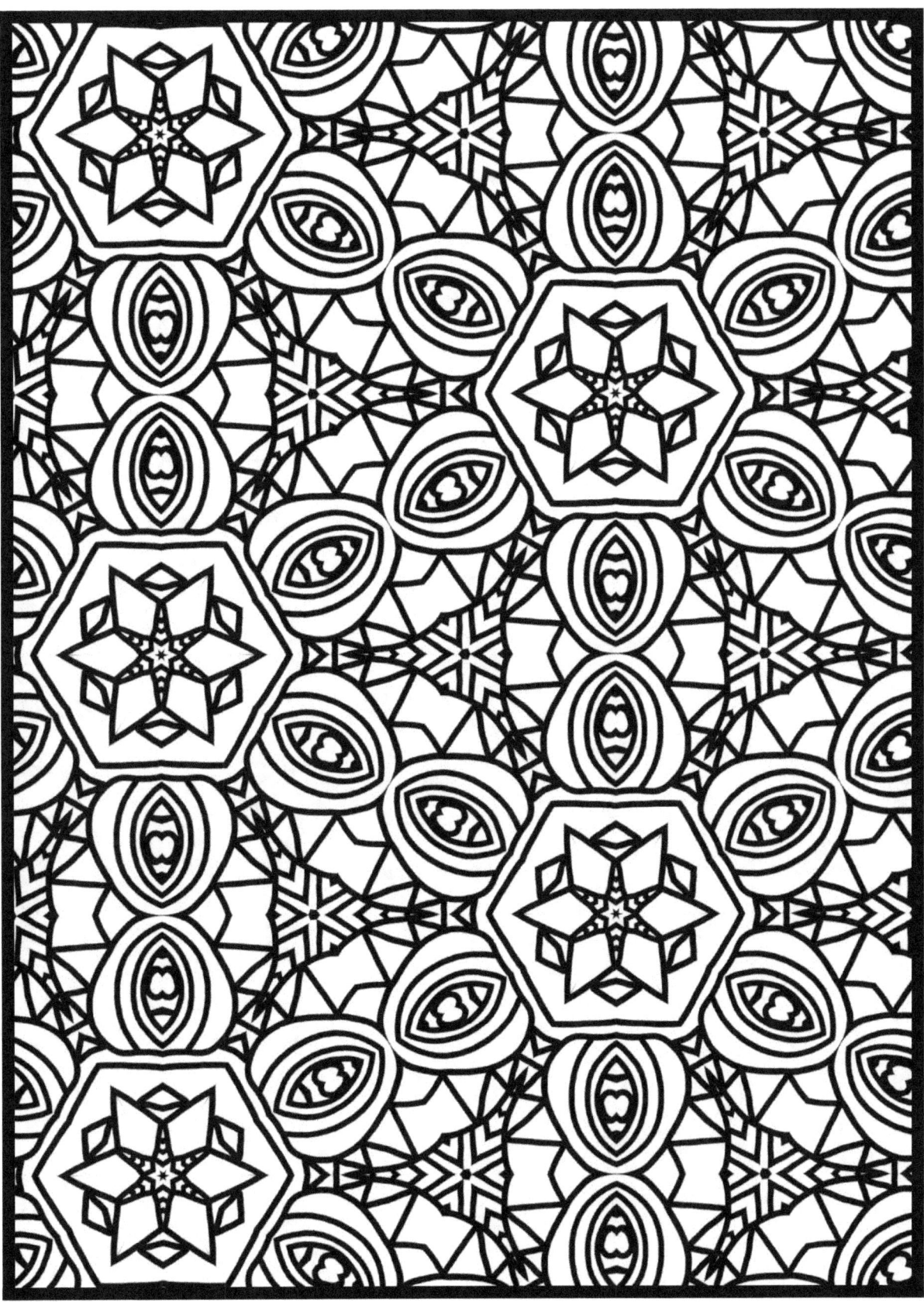

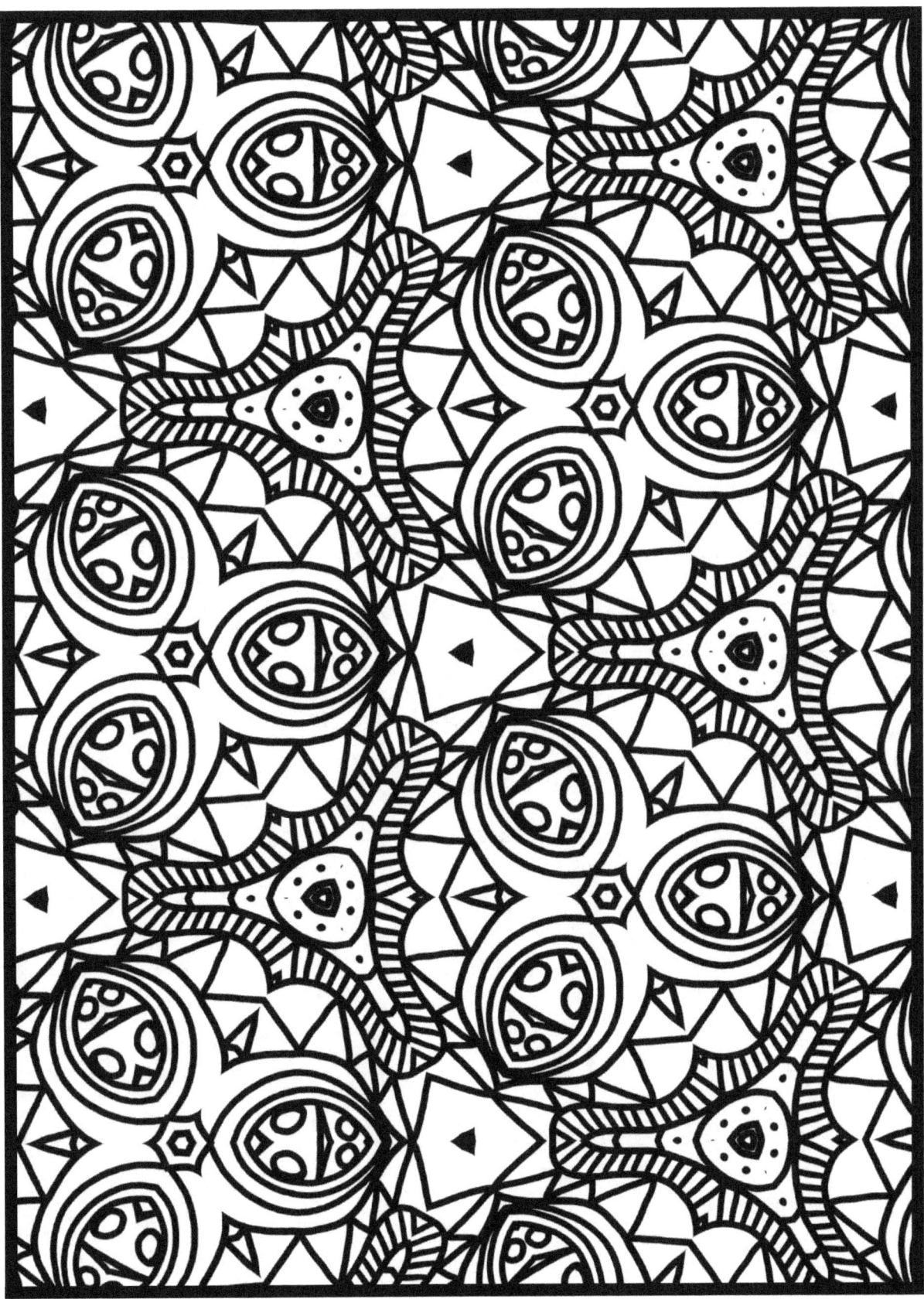

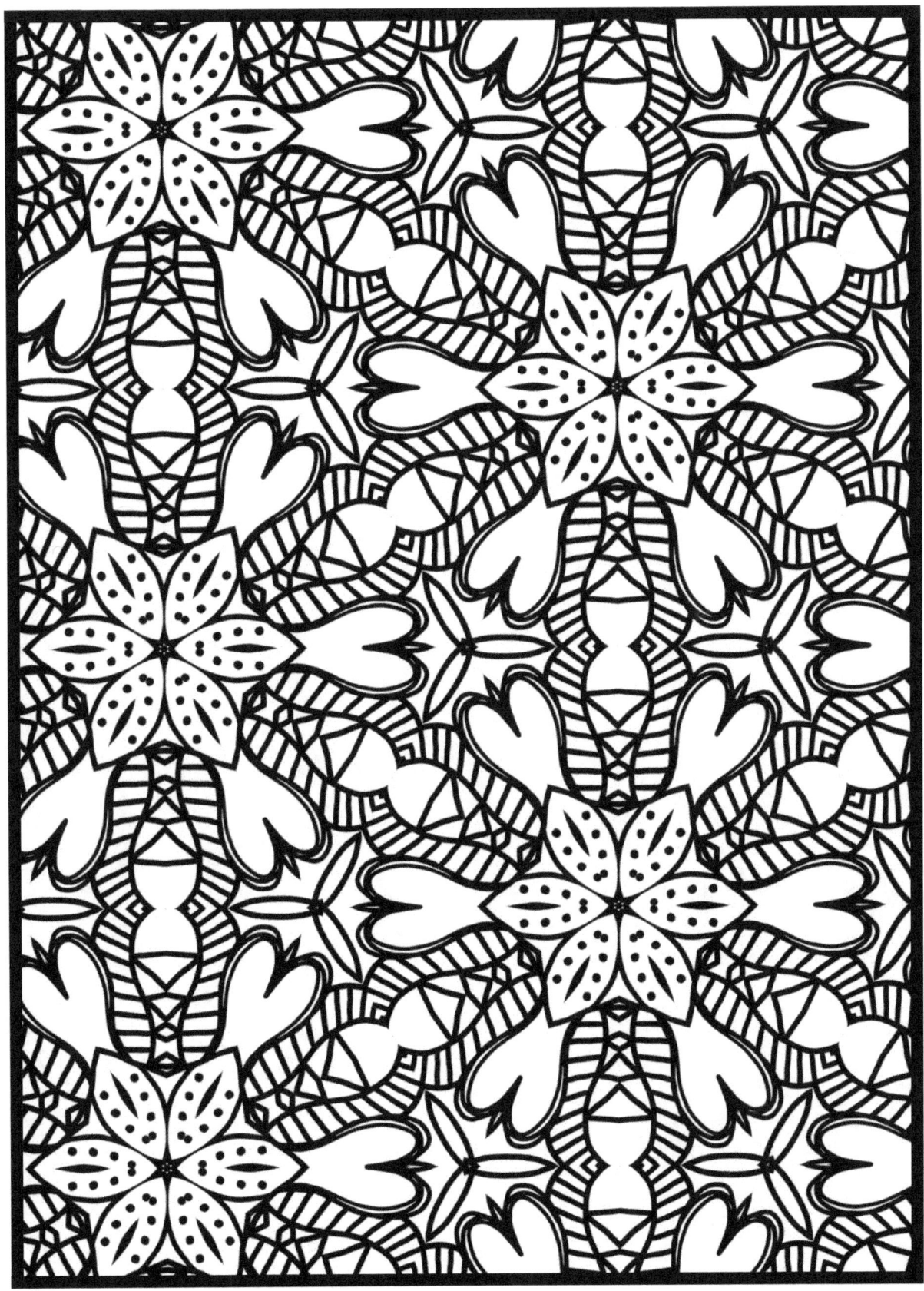

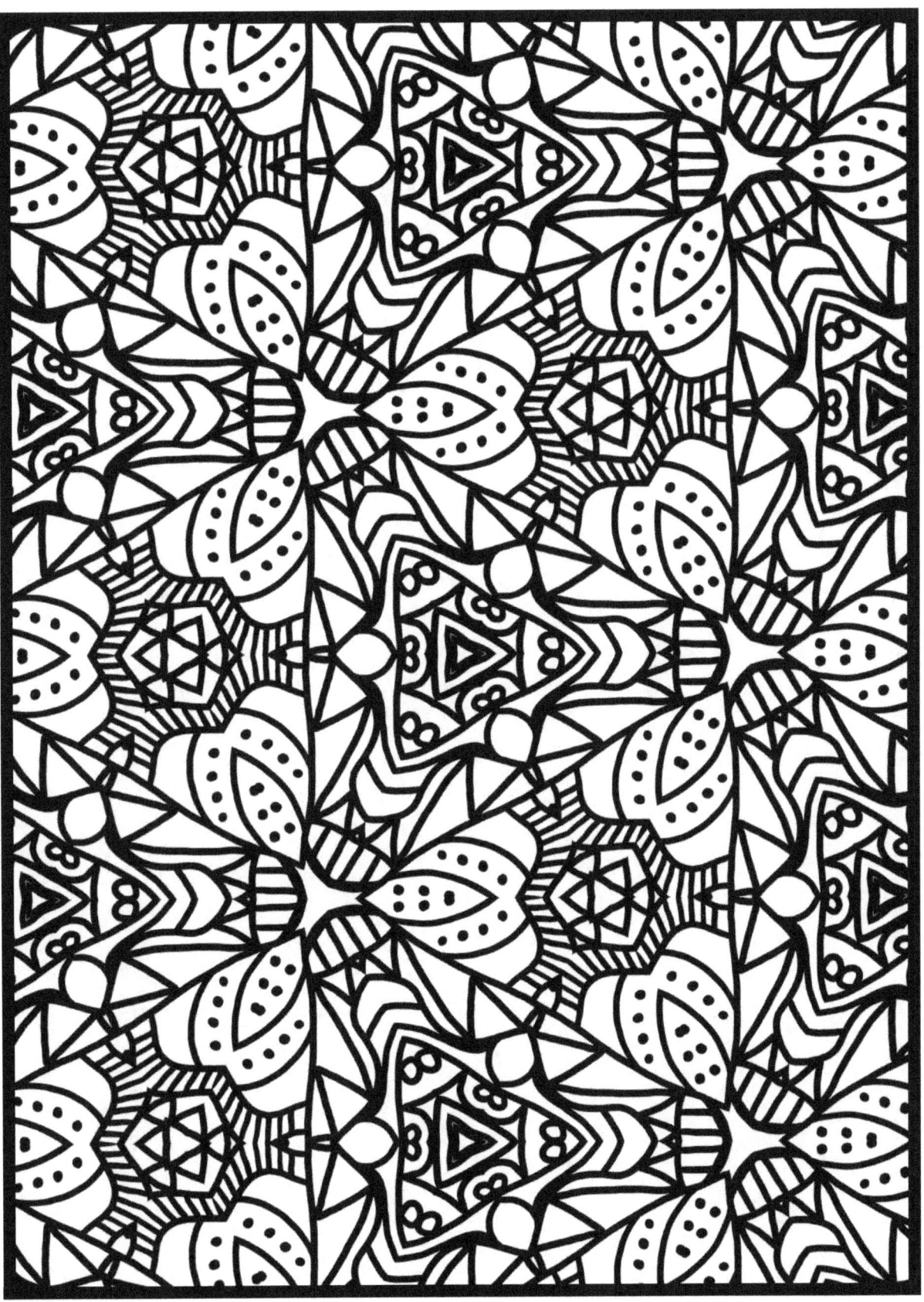

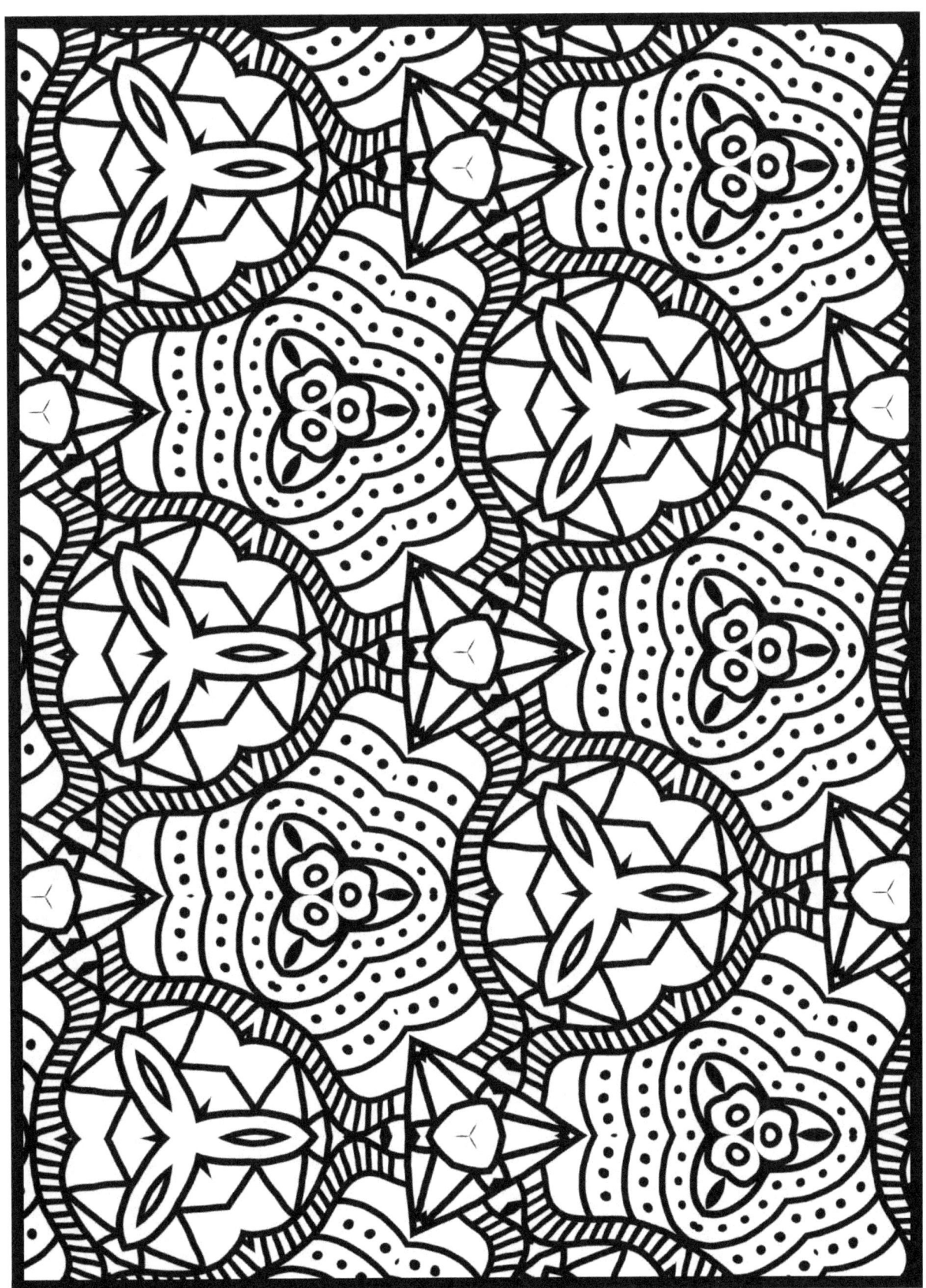

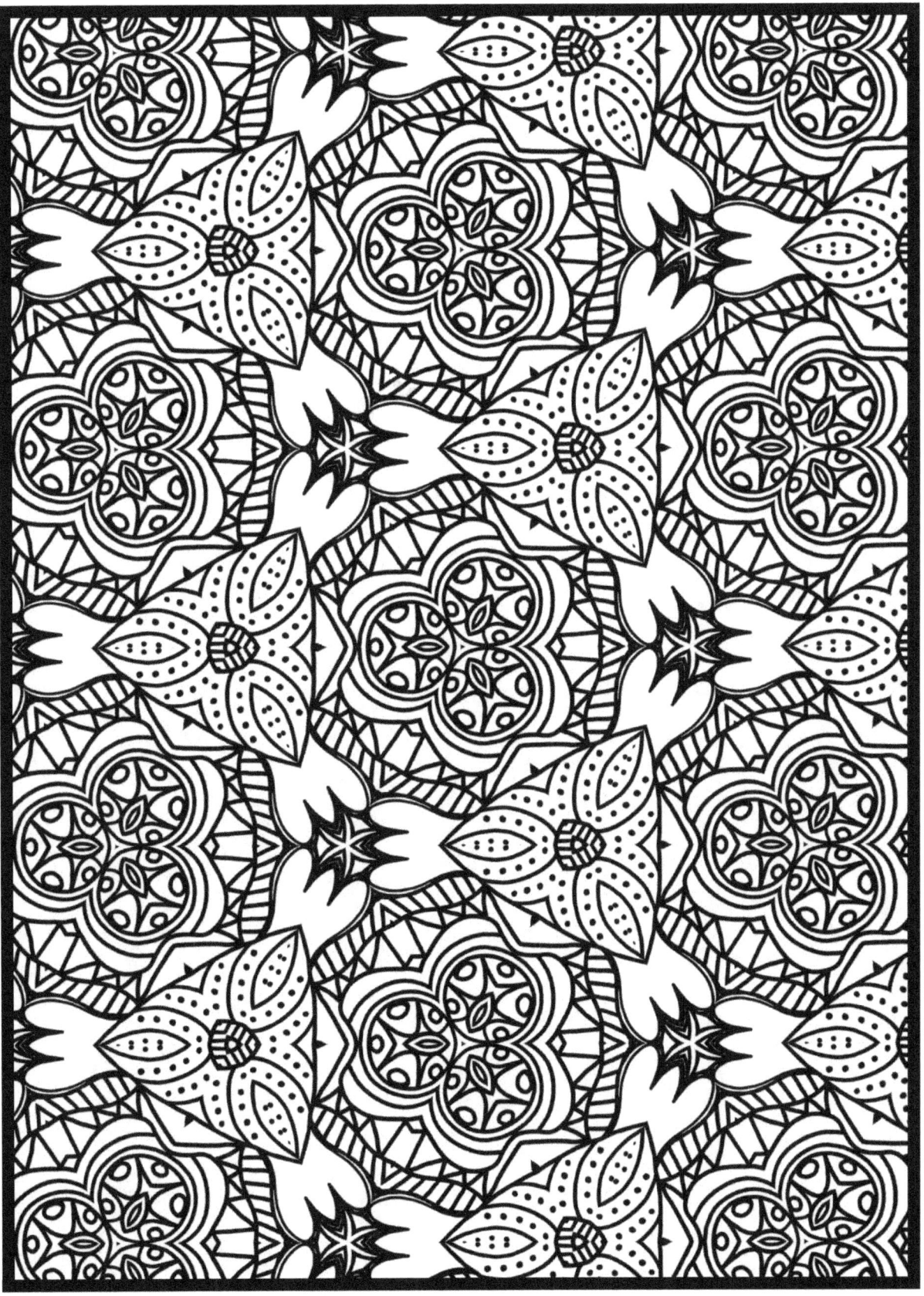

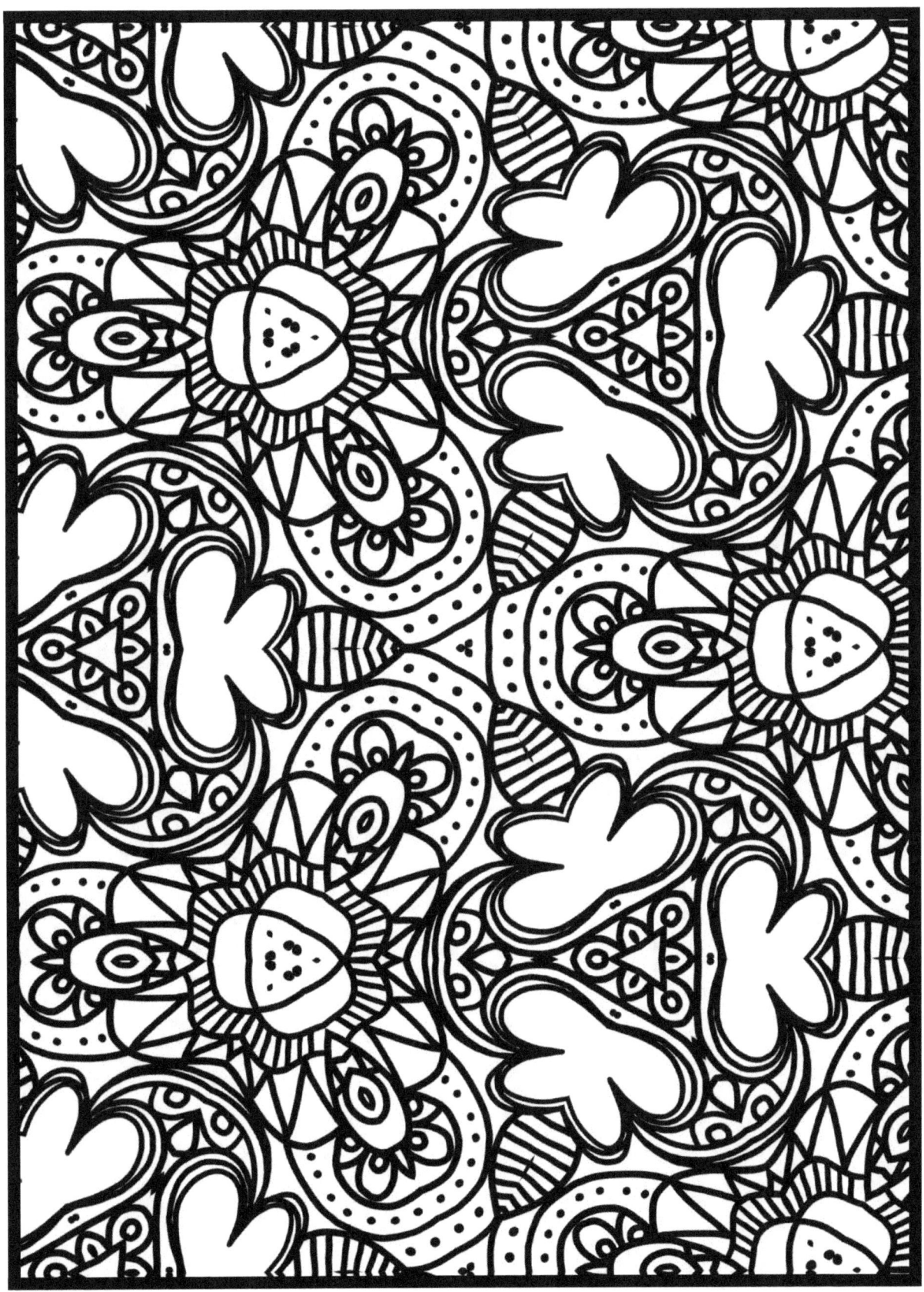

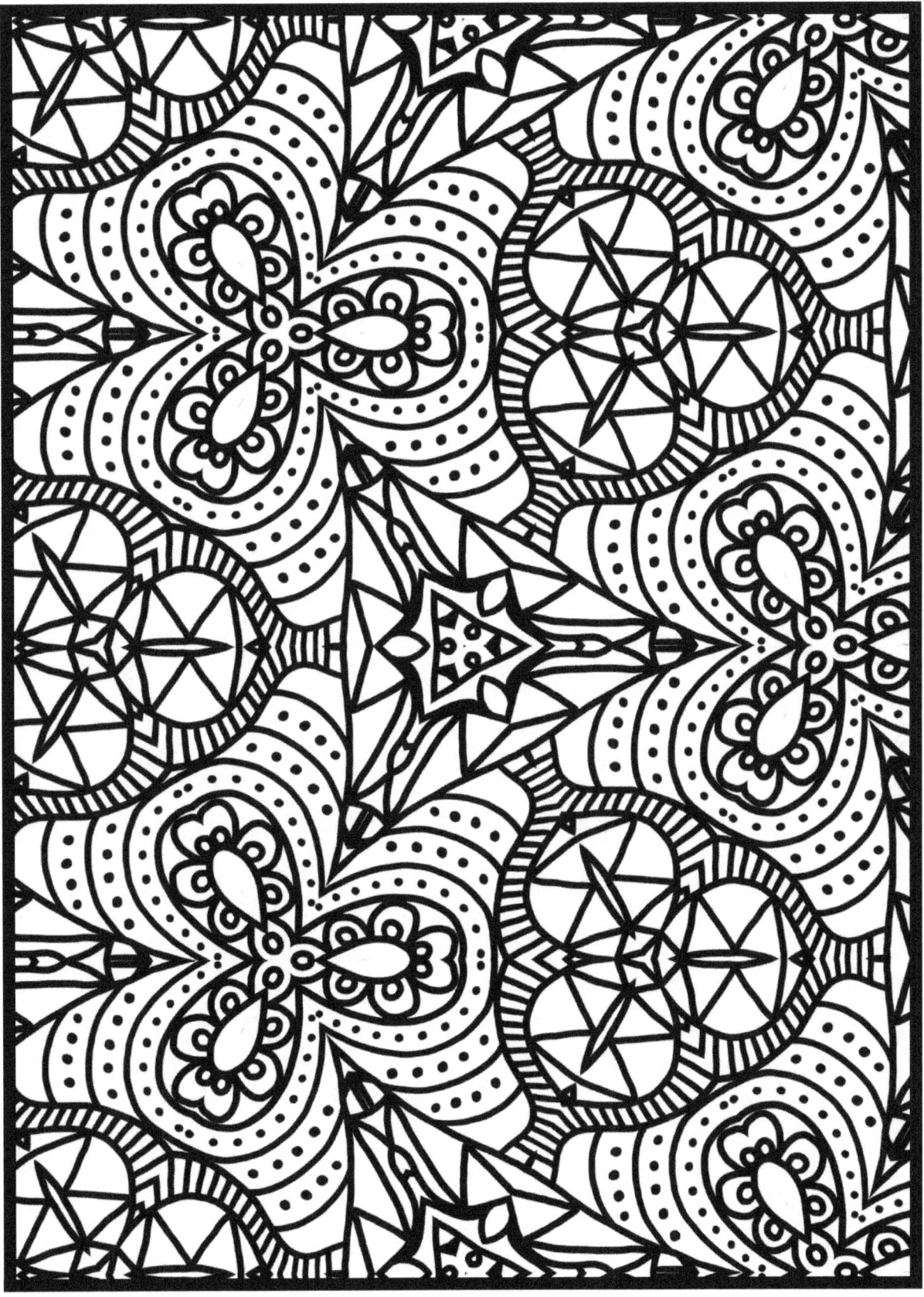

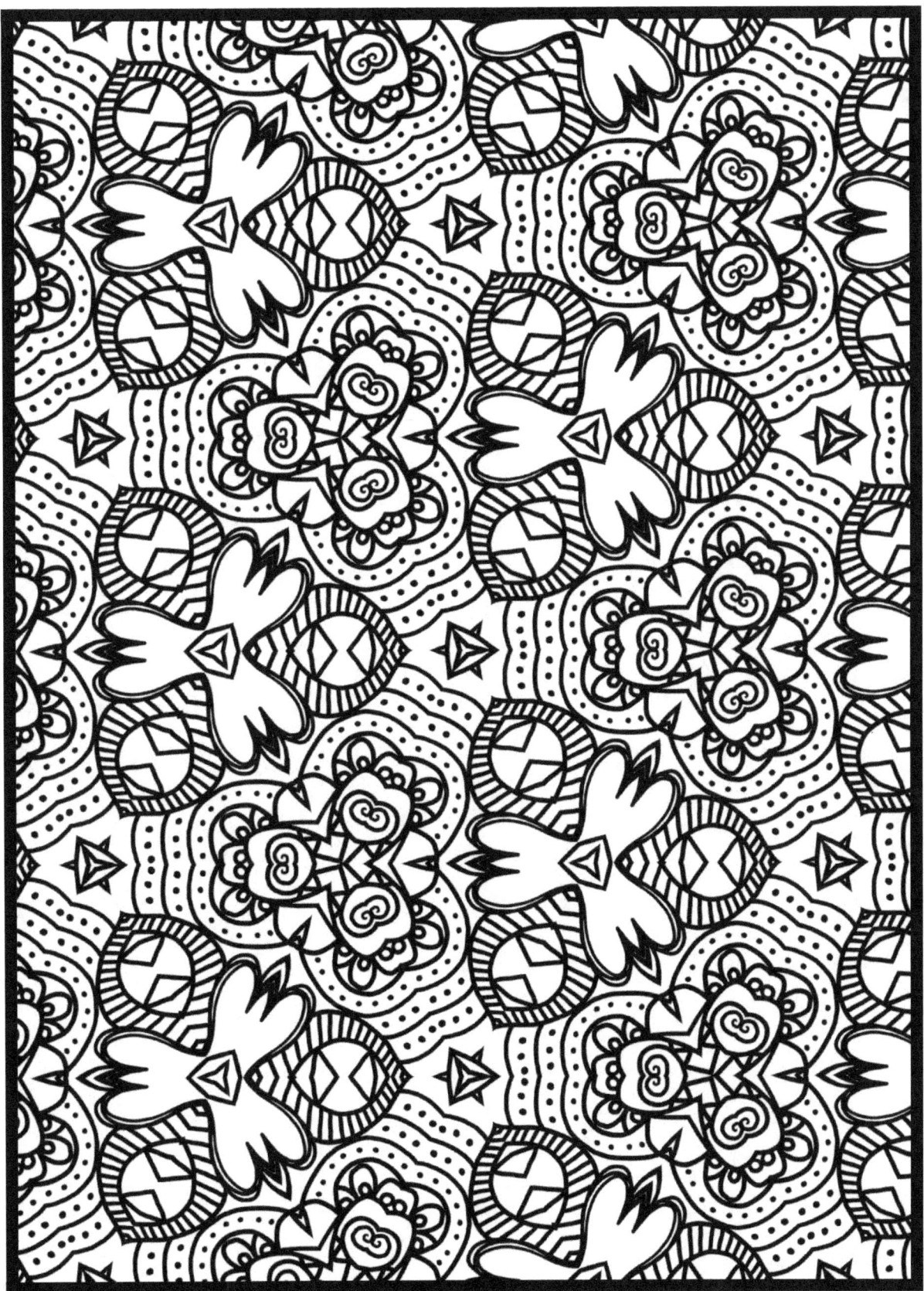

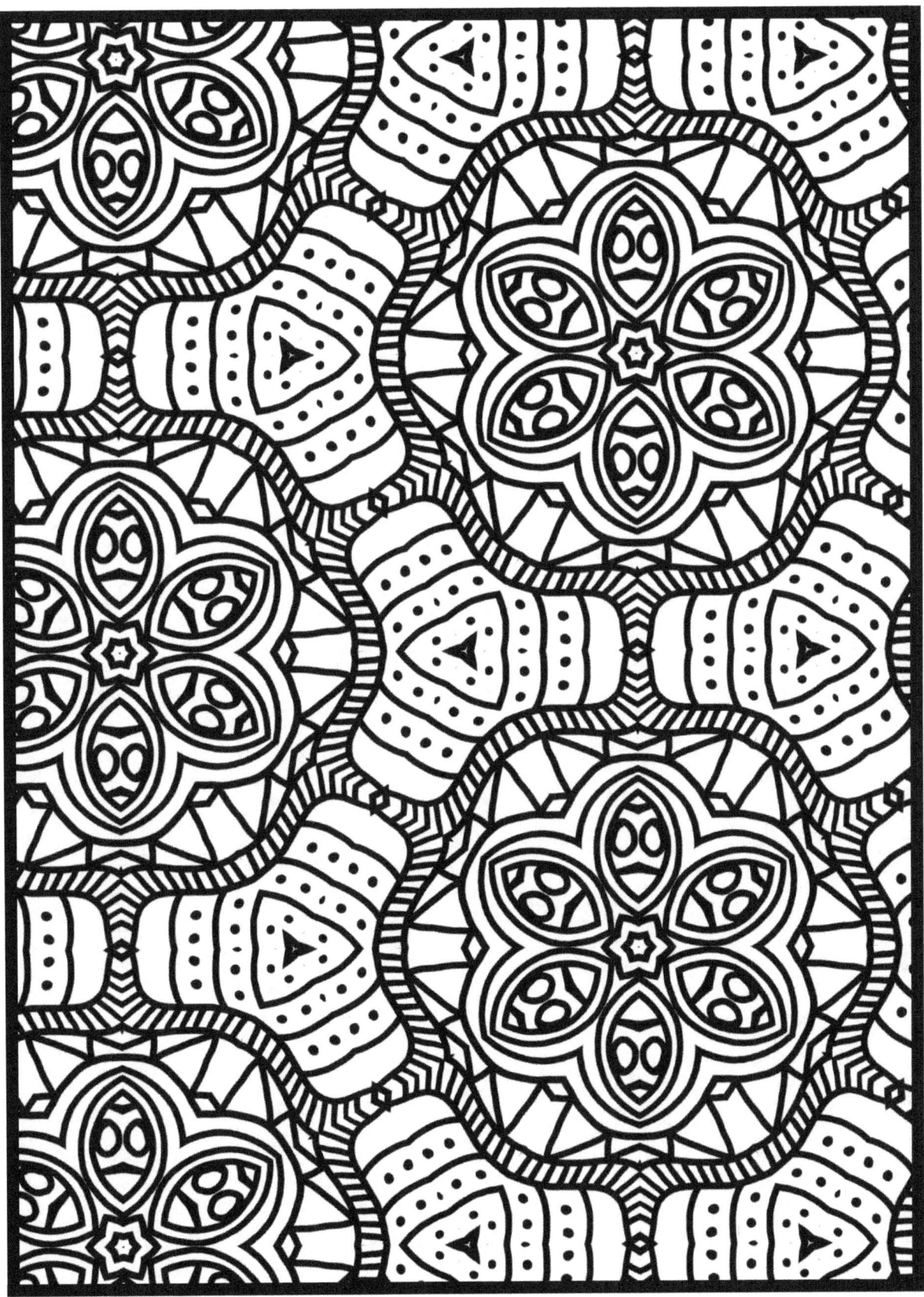

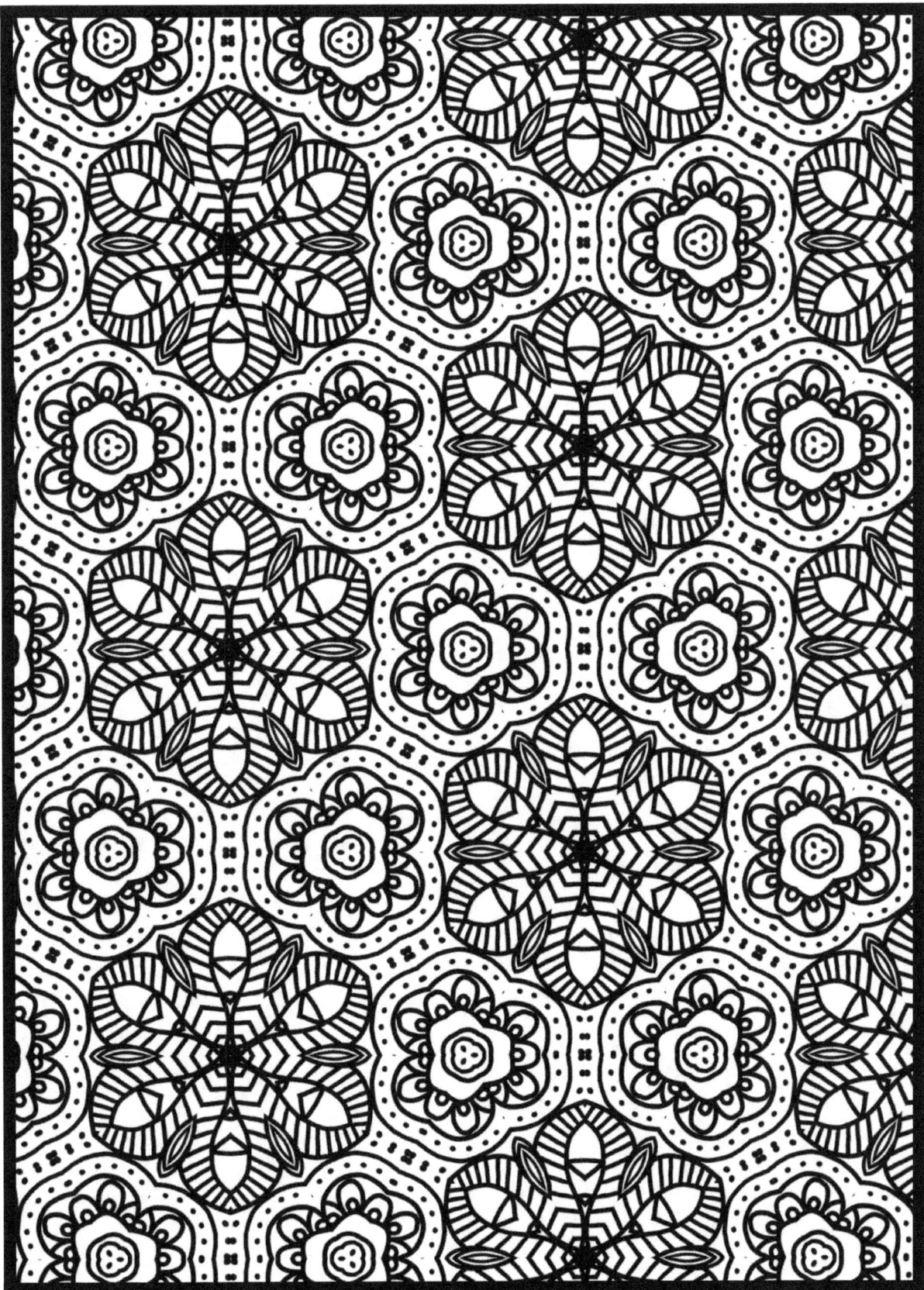

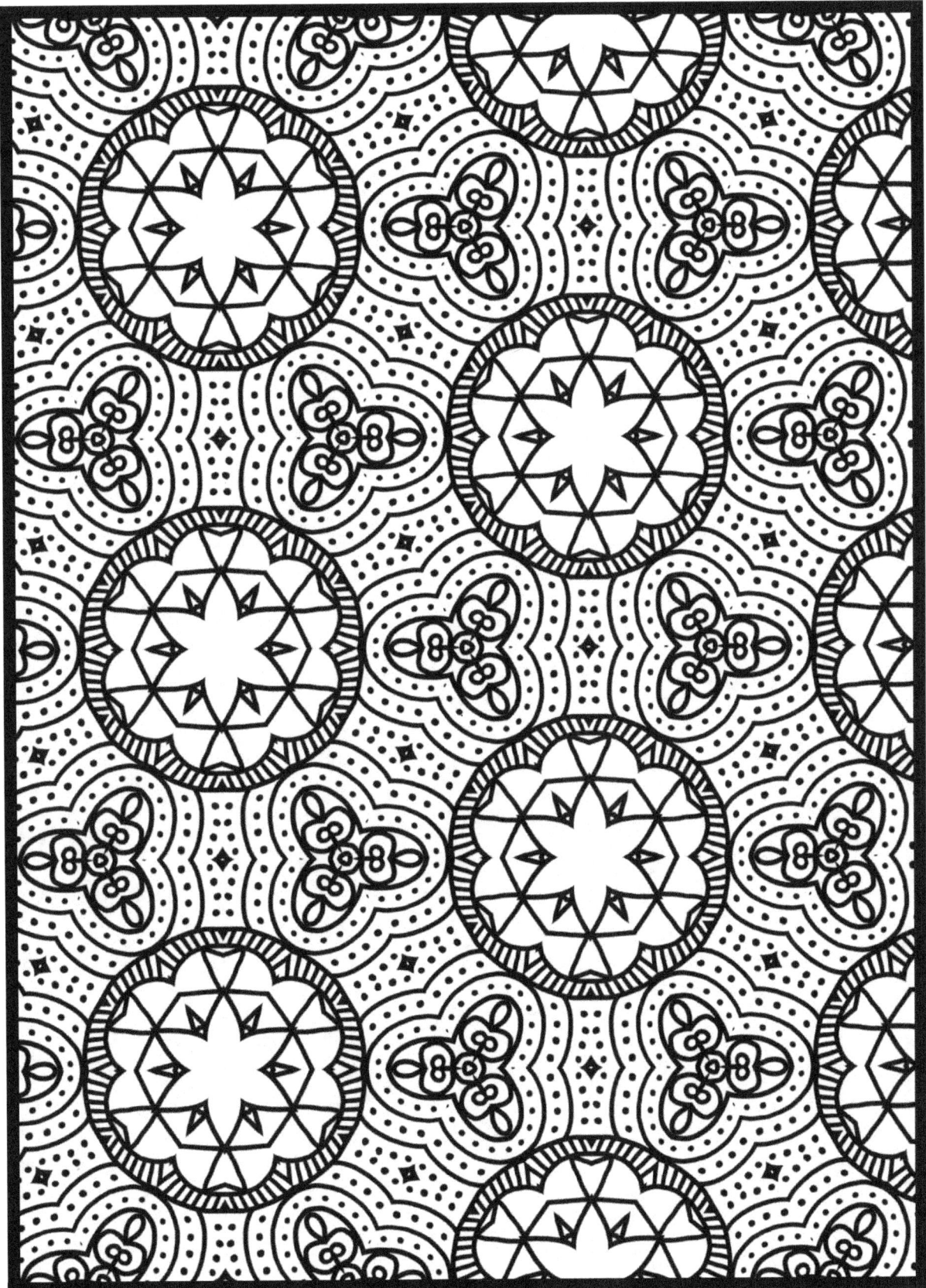

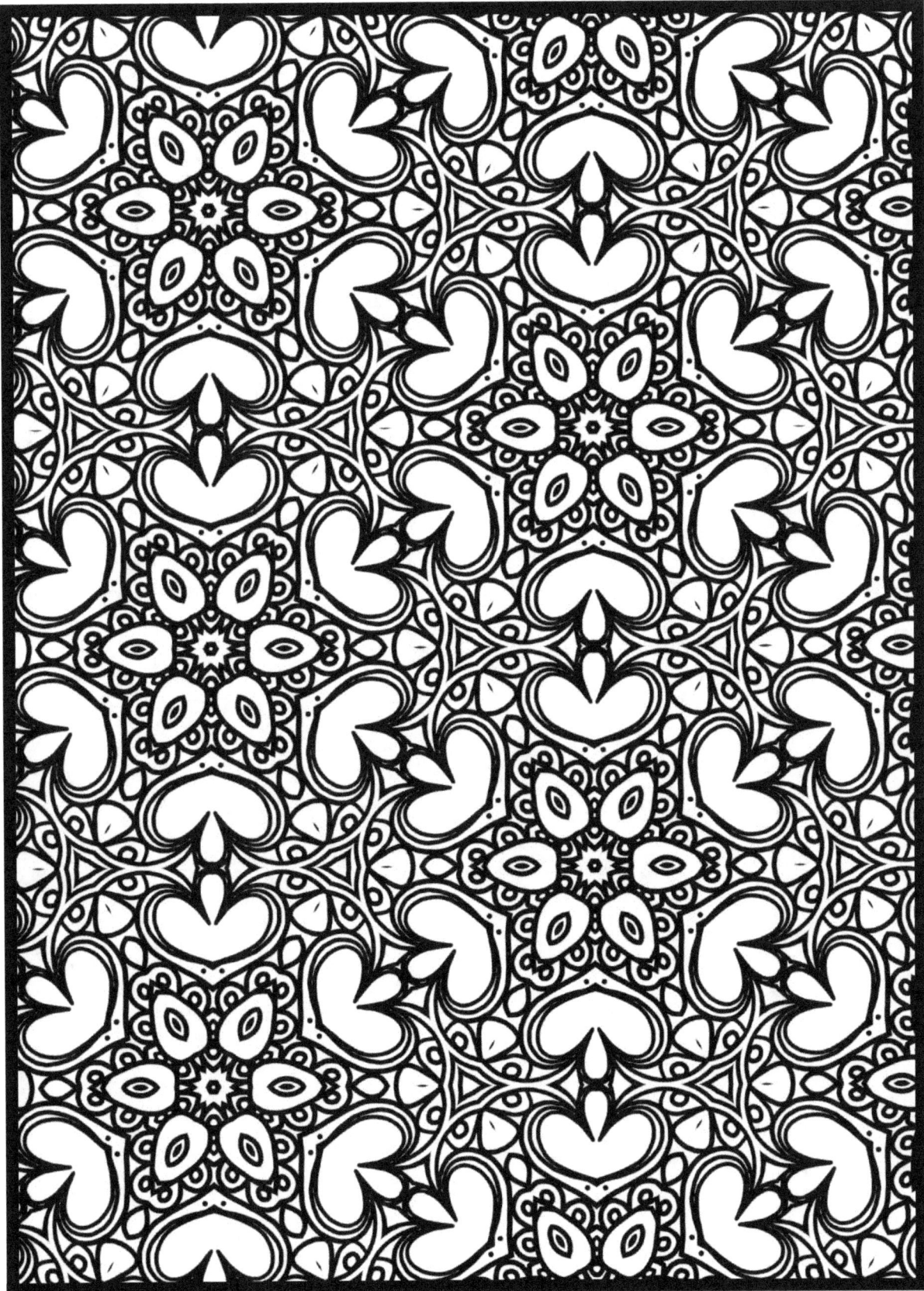

About the Author

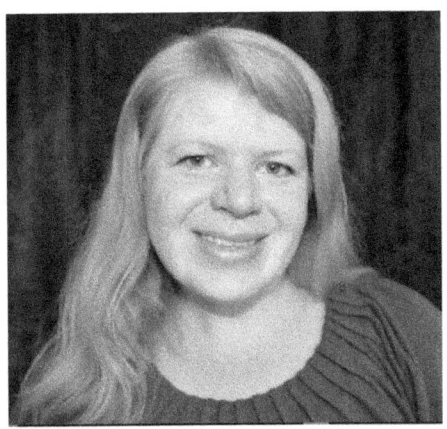

Star Miller-Becerra

Star is a mother of 2 children, married and lives just outside of Washington, DC in Maryland. She loves putting smiles on others faces, volunteering in schools and in the community.

Spending quality family time together is very important to her and she enjoys traveling as much as possible. Most of her family lives thousands of miles away - all across the United States, and her in-laws live in Panama. She enjoys learning new Spanish words and phrases every day.

Coloring is very therapeutic, and allows Star to get into her creative zone. She created "Color More & Stress Less" while coloring with her children. Her hope is that you make coloring a family thing as well. You'd be surprised as to what conversations come out of children's mouths while they are in their creative zone - Priceless!

Visit us for free coloring page downloads and more:

www.colormorestressless.com

www.ingramcontent.com/pod-product-compliance
Lightning Source LLC
Chambersburg PA
CBHW080551190526
45169CB00007B/2731